This book belongs to

Age

Favourite player

Prediction of Birmingham's final position this season

Prediction of Barclays Premier League winners this season

Prediction of FA Cup winners this season

Prediction of Carling Cup winners this season

Prediction of teams to be relegated
from the Barclays Premier League this season:

18th

19th

20th

Written by Twocan

A TWOCAN PUBLICATION

©2010. Published by Twocan
under licence from Birmingham City FC.

Every effort has been made to ensure the accuracy of
information within this publication but the publishers can
not be held responsible for any errors or omissions.

Views expressed are those of the author and do not
necessarily represent those of the publishers or the
football club.

ISBN 978-0-9559299-7-7

PICTURE CREDITS
Press Association

£6.99

Contents

St. Andrew's
HOME OF THE BLUES

A

The Blues moved to St. Andrew's in 1906 from their first ground, Muntz Street.

The first game was played against Middlesbrough in December 1906. The game attracted a crowd of 32,000 and ended 0-0!

During the First World War Blues were asked to help the cause by offering the use of St. Andrew's as a rifle range to train the soldiers!

The 1925-26 season saw the first visit of foreign opposition at St. Andrew's. Real Madrid were beaten 3-0 in a friendly.

The Blues pitch measures 100m by 66m

St.Andrew's
...interesting!

During the World War Two, the stadium was bombed and, until the ground was restored, the Blues had to play home games at Villa Park

...the home of their arch-rivals Aston Villa!

The record attendance is 66,844
v Everton · FA Cup Round 5 · 11 March 1939

The current ground capacity is 30,009

Beau's Buddies
(0-8 years) and
Blues Crew
(9-16 years)
are the official junior
membership clubs for
Birmingham City FC

BIRMINGHAM CITY
FOOTBALL CLUB
- 1875 -

B | The Blues OFFICIAL JUNIOR CLUBS

Membership to the clubs is totally free and once registered members will receive a welcome letter, giant fun poster-magazine and an official membership card with 10%* discount in the Blues Superstore.

Members will receive unlimited access to the fun websites with all the latest news from the club, match reports, games, quizzes and competitions with fantastic prizes, interactive polls, pictures and video galleries, downloadable wallpapers and a 'Your Shout!' section to see your letters, pictures and photos on screen.

Plus, members will also receive monthly emails straight to their inboxes and invites to member only player attended events. Members who attend three or more of these events and get their membership cards stamped, will be promoted to the exclusive Gold Membership club!

**Register for free at
www.beaus-buddies.com
or www.blues-crew.com.**

*EXCLUDES XTEP PRODUCTS.

PLAYER NAME: Enric Valles CLUB

POSITION: Midfielder

SQUAD NUMBER: 20

DATE OF BIRTH: 1st March 1990

BIRTHPLACE: Barcelona, Spain

Born in Barcelona, Valles is a graduate of the illustrious FC Barcelona youth system.

The 6ft 2in left-midfielder moved to Dutch side NAC Breda in 2008 and enjoyed a two year spell in the Netherlands before leaving the club at the end 2009-10 season.

The Blues snapped Valles up as a free agent in the summer 2010 on a one-year deal and Alex McLeish predicts a big future for the tricky player, describing him as a "very good footballer".

BIRMINGHAM CITY
FOOTBALL CLUB
- 1875 -

NAME: **Enric Valles**
POSITION: Midfielder
SQUAD NUMBER: 20

1

TO WATCH
One

A

B

C

D

E

F

BIRMINGHAM CITY
FOOTBALL CLUB
- 1875 -

C | CLUB CREST TEST

Can you name the Barclays Premier
League Clubs that these crests belong to?

Birmingham City
BARCLAYS PREMIER LEAGUE SQUAD

BIRMINGHAM CITY FOOTBALL CLUB
- 1875 -

TOP ROW (L-R): Dr Ian McGuinness (Chief Medical Officer), David Murphy, Marcus Bent, Cameron Jerome, Liam Ridgewell, Scott Dann, Nikola Zigic, Roger Johnson, Garry O'Connor, Enric Valles, Pete Shaw (First team Physiotherapist).
MIDDLE ROW: Nick Davies (Head of Sport Science), Dave Watson (Goalkeeping Coach), Keith Fahey, Barry Ferguson, Lee Bowyer, Maik Taylor, Ben Foster, Colin Doyle, Stuart Parnaby, Michel, Craig Gardner, George Cooper (First team Physiotherapist), Andy Kalinins (Sports Science).
FRONT ROW: Dave Hunt (First team Physiotherapist), Paul Doherty (Masseur), Jonathan Seeley (Masseur), Matt Derbyshire, Stephen Carr, Seb Larsson, Peter Grant (First Team Coach), Alex McLeish (First Team Manager), Andy Watson (First team Coach), Jay O'Shea, James McFadden, Kevin Phillips, Denis Butler (Kit Manager), Joe Carnall (Performance Analyst), Paul Carter (Assistant Kit Manager).

10·11

ALEXANDER HLEB

JEAN BEAUSEJOUR

MARTIN JIRANEK

BIRMINGHAM CITY FOOTBALL CLUB - 1875 -

D

SCOTT Dann

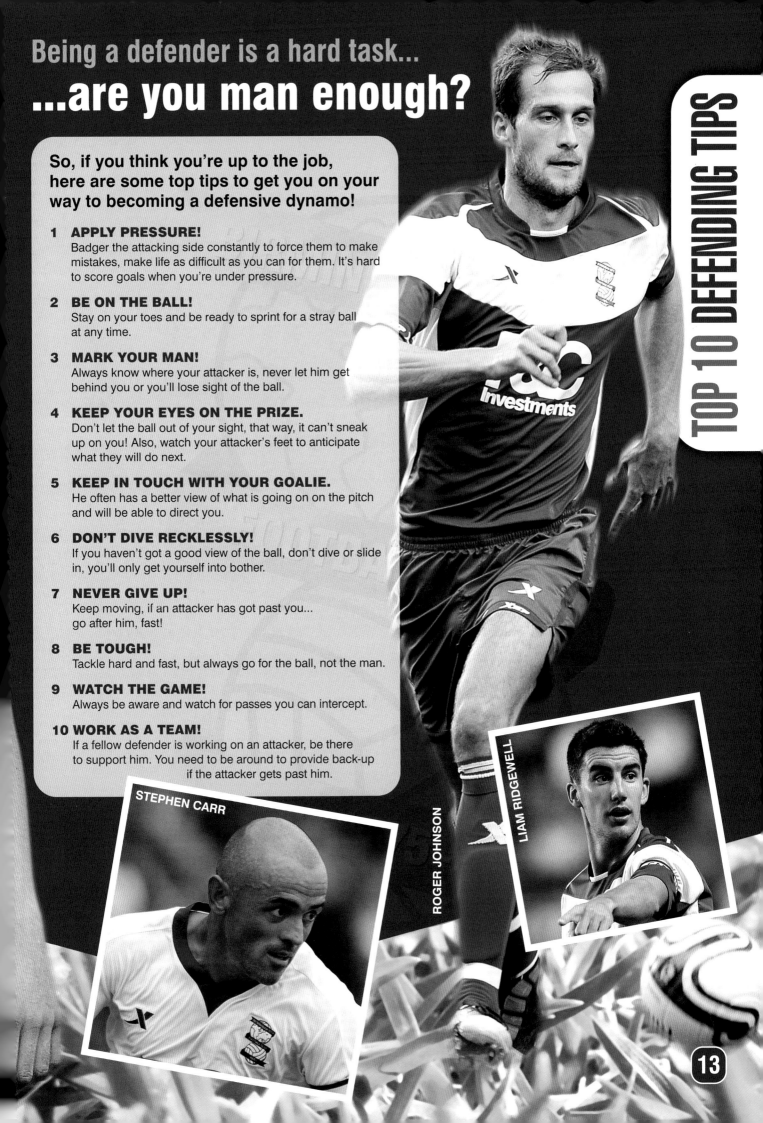

Being a defender is a hard task...
...are you man enough?

So, if you think you're up to the job, here are some top tips to get you on your way to becoming a defensive dynamo!

1 APPLY PRESSURE!
Badger the attacking side constantly to force them to make mistakes, make life as difficult as you can for them. It's hard to score goals when you're under pressure.

2 BE ON THE BALL!
Stay on your toes and be ready to sprint for a stray ball at any time.

3 MARK YOUR MAN!
Always know where your attacker is, never let him get behind you or you'll lose sight of the ball.

4 KEEP YOUR EYES ON THE PRIZE.
Don't let the ball out of your sight, that way, it can't sneak up on you! Also, watch your attacker's feet to anticipate what they will do next.

5 KEEP IN TOUCH WITH YOUR GOALIE.
He often has a better view of what is going on on the pitch and will be able to direct you.

6 DON'T DIVE RECKLESSLY!
If you haven't got a good view of the ball, don't dive or slide in, you'll only get yourself into bother.

7 NEVER GIVE UP!
Keep moving, if an attacker has got past you... go after him, fast!

8 BE TOUGH!
Tackle hard and fast, but always go for the ball, not the man.

9 WATCH THE GAME!
Always be aware and watch for passes you can intercept.

10 WORK AS A TEAM!
If a fellow defender is working on an attacker, be there to support him. You need to be around to provide back-up if the attacker gets past him.

STEPHEN CARR

ROGER JOHNSON

LIAM RIDGEWELL

Stars in their eyes

CAN YOU IDENTIFY THE EIGHT BLUES STARS

14

ANSWERS ON PAGE 62.

BIRMINGHAM CITY
FOOTBALL CLUB
- 1875 -

F

POSITION: Midfielder
SQUAD NUMBER: 12

BARRY
Ferguson

Fan'tastic

ANSWERS ON PAGE 62.

BIRMINGHAM CITY
FOOTBALL CLUB
- 1875 -

F

There are five famous sportsmen hidden in the crowd.
Can you find them all?

17

BIRMINGHAM CITY FOOTBALL CLUB · 1875

G

THE Gaffer

- Alex grew up a Rangers fan but signed for Aberdeen in 1976 where he made 493 of his 496 league appearances!

- **He enjoyed great success at Aberdeen under the management of Alex Ferguson, including winning several Scottish Premier League titles, Scottish Cups and a European Cup Winners' Cup medal when 'The Dons' beat Real Madrid 2·1 in 1983**

- When Ferguson left to go to Manchester United in 1986, he tried to get Alex to sign without success. He also had talks with Tottenham Hotspur.

- **Was 'Scottish Player of the Year' in 1990**

- He played in three World Cups with Scotland, in 1982, 1986 and 1990

- **Alex won 77 international caps in total**

- Even after he had won his first Scotland cap, Alex McLeish's father asked then Aberdeen boss Alex Ferguson to persuade him to continue training as an accountant!

Alex won his first game as Birmingham manager, on 2 December 2007, winning 3·2 against Spurs at White Hart Lane

- McLeish's first managerial role was at Motherwell where he took over from Tommy McLean as player manager in 1994

- **He made just 3 appearances on the field as a player for the club**

- In his first season at Motherwell he guided the club to second in the Scottish Premier League behind Rangers

- **McLeish was appointed manager of a struggling Hibernian side in 1998, which was relegated from the Scottish Premier Division that season despite a slight upturn in fortunes under McLeish**

- However, he guided the Edinburgh team back to the Scottish Premier League at the first attempt by winning the First Division title the following season

- **In his third season, McLeish's Hibs finished third behind Celtic and Rangers in the league and made it to the Scottish Cup Final**

- He was linked with several clubs in England, before he was appointed as Rangers manager in December 2001

- **He was hugely successful at Rangers, winning 2 Scottish Premier Leagues, 2 Scottish Cups and 3 Scottish League Cups and took the club to the knockout stages of the Champions League for the first time**

- After leaving Rangers, he spent 10 months as Scotland manager before joining The Blues in November 2007

- **The 2009-10 season saw McLeish lead the Blues to ninth spot, their best ever finish in the Barclays Premier League**

- In recognition of his distinguished service to Scottish sport, in 2008 McLeish was awarded an honorary doctorate by the University of Aberdeen

Alex is a member of Scottish Football's Hall of Fame

Healthy EATING

H

A healthy and balanced diet is recommended for everyone but for a professional footballer it is crucial.

Players must eat the right balance of starchy foods, fruit and vegetables, dairy foods, meat, fish, fats and sugar to help keep their bodies strong, energized, and well nourished.

The Birmingham City FC catering team ensure that they provide the players with a wide selection of foods at Wast Hills training ground to help them refuel after a hard work-out.

On match days, the Blues chefs prepare the right balance of foods for pre-match meals so that the players have maximum energy when they step out onto the pitch.

SAMPLE MENU

Starters

Tomato and Onion Salad with light dressing

Tuna with kidney beans in olive oil

Leak and Potato Soup

Mains

Chicken Pasta Bake

Beef and Vegetable Stir Fry

Salmon Steaks with Steamed Rice

Desserts

Fresh Fruit Cocktail

Rice Pudding

2

Two Blues Stars are mixed up
in each of these head shots?
Can you identify them?

TAKE 2

ANSWERS ON PAGE 62.

Sebastian
Larsson

James McFadden

DIADORA

Ben Foster

Kevin Phillips

Barry Ferguson

DIADORA

BELARUS

CHILE

CZECH REPUBLIC

ENGLAND

NORTHERN IRELAND

REPUBLIC OF IRELAND

SCOTLAND

SERBIA

SWEDEN

22

ANSWERS ON PAGE 62.

Stephen Carr

Garry O'Connor

Keith Fahey

Can you match the Blues Star
to the Country they have represented?

Write the players name next to their nation's flag.

Nikola Zigic

Lee Bowyer

Maik Taylor

Stars

INTERNATIONAL

Colin Doyle

Martin Jiranek

Joan Beausejour

Alexander Hleb

23

BIRMINGHAM CITY
FOOTBALL CLUB
- 1875 -

POSITION: Striker
SQUAD NUMBER: 10

J

CAMERON
Jerome

Being a keeper is a tough job...
...but someone's gotta do it!

So, if you think you're man enough for the challenge, here are some top tips to get you on track for becoming an all star keeper!

1 KEEP MOVING AND STAY ON YOUR TOES!
A good goalie's feet are constantly moving and ready for anything that's coming their way. Never sit back on your heels, that's when you'll make mistakes.

2 SHOUT... LOUD!
You have to communicate with your team, let them know when you need help or when you think they need to be watching opposing players.

3 STAY LOOSE AND RELAXED.
If you're tense, diving and getting hit with the ball will hurt more.

4 STAY AWAKE!
You've got to be watching the game all the time in order to be ready to step up when it's your turn to shine. Remember, it only takes seconds for the game to change completely.

5 WATCH PLAYERS' FEET.
The way their feet are positioned when going to take a kick can indicate where the ball is going.

6 BOUNCE BACK!
After diving your length for a ball, recover quickly, play doesn't stop because you're on the ground.

7 STAY SQUARE TO THE BALL.
At all times, keep your hips and shoulders pointed towards the shooter.

8 TREAT ALL SHOTS WITH RESPECT!
No matter how soft the shot or how easy the save, always make the effort to get the ball under full control. It's when you get lazy that mistakes happen.

9 HAVE AN INSURANCE POLICY!
Always have a part of your body behind the ball as well as your hands. That way, if the ball slips through your fingers, your body will be there to stop it.

10 HAVE COURAGE!
Take pride in your position as your team's last defender and have confidence in yourself. You have to put yourself in positions where you might end up getting hit but it's these saves that win matches.

BEN FOSTER

COLIN DOYLE

MAIK TAYLOR

NAME: Gilbert Harold Merrick
BORN: Birmingham · 26.01.1922
DIED: 03.02.2010

BIRMINGHAM CITY
FOOTBALL CLUB
- 1875 -

L

There's only one word to describe Gil Merrick, Birmingham City's all-time record appearance maker and longest-serving player **...Legend!**

GIL Merrick

Proud to sponsor The Blues

F&C Investments

GIL MERRICK 1922-2010

In recognition of his service to Blues, in 2009 the club renamed the Railway Stand at St Andrew's the Gil Merrick Stand.

LEAGUE CUP LEGENDS

The keeper who signed for Blues in 1938 clocked up a total of 551 league appearances for City as well as appearing in over 170 matches during the Second World War.

Merrick's superb ability between the sticks also earned him 23 caps for England.

He finally hung up his playing boots in 1960, a remarkable 22 years after starting his career with the Blues.

Merrick then went on to manage the Blues for four years, during which time the clubs won their only major honour to date - as League Cup winners in 1963, a victory made even sweeter as it was against arch rivals Aston Villa!

A true Blues Legend!

Can you work out the identity of these five Birmingham stars?

BIRMINGHAM CITY FOOTBALL CLUB - 1875 -

M

A

B

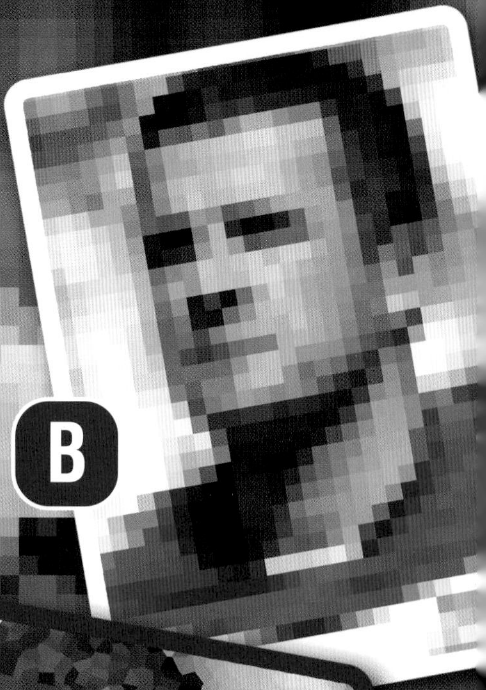

C

D

E

MEGA Pixels

ANSWERS ON PAGE 62.

Joe Bradford
Birmingham City · 1920-1935

3

Joe Bradford, the Blues all time record goalscorer who amassed 267 goals in 445 appearances for the club also holds the record for the most hat-tricks for City.

He scored an amazing 13 hat-tricks over his Birmingham career - 12 in the league and 1 in the FA Cup.

Bradford who played for Blues between 1920 and 1935 was one of the finest forwards of his generation.

He was lightening fast with the ability to strike the ball with either foot, as well as a great header of the ball.

NAME: **Ben Foster**
POSITION: Goalkeeper
SQUAD NUMBER: 26

N

MEET THE New

DATE OF BIRTH: 3rd April 1983
BIRTHPLACE: Leamington Spa, England
SIGNED FROM: Manchester United
INTERNATIONAL: England

PLAYER NAME: Martin Jiranek
POSITION: Defender
SQUAD NUMBER: 28
DATE OF BIRTH: 25th May 1979
BIRTHPLACE: Prague, Czechoslovakia
SIGNED FROM: Spartak Moscow
INTERNATIONAL: Czech Republic

Matt Derbyshire
POSITION: **Striker**
SQUAD NUMBER: **14**

PLAYER NAME: Nikola Zigic
POSITION: Striker
SQUAD NUMBER: 19
DATE OF BIRTH: 25th September 1980
BIRTHPLACE: Backa Topola, Serbia
SIGNED FROM: Valencia
INTERNATIONAL: Serbia

PLAYER NAME: Jean Beausejour
POSITION: Midfielder
SQUAD NUMBER: 23
DATE OF BIRTH: 1st June 1984
BIRTHPLACE: Santiago, Chile
SIGNED FROM: Club America
INTERNATIONAL: Chile

Blues

DATE OF BIRTH: 14th April 1986
BIRTHPLACE: Blackburn, England
SIGNED FROM: Olympiakos (loan)
INTERNATIONAL: England U21

PLAYER NAME: Alexander Hleb
POSITION: Midfielder
SQUAD NUMBER: 22
DATE OF BIRTH: 1st May 1981
BIRTHPLACE: Minsk, Belarus
SIGNED FROM: Barcelona (loan)
INTERNATIONAL: Belarus

BIRMINGHAM CITY
FOOTBALL CLUB
- 1875 -

0

GARRY
O'Connor

BIRMINGHAM CITY
FOOTBALL CLUB
- 1875 -

P

Can you finish this picture of Garry O'Connor? ...and colour it in?

PICTURE
Perfect

FOUR STEPS TO...

4

STAGE 1
EASY PEASY

1 All you need is a football and some cones to mark out a goal

2 Take ten steps back and practice shooting into different parts of the goal

3 Aim for different parts of the goal so that every penalty is different

STAGE 2
MEDIUM

1 Ask a friend to join you

2 Tell your friend where you are going to put your shot, then go for it

3 This makes it more of a challenge and so helps you improve

Perfect Penalty

STAGE 3
TOUGH

1 Ask your friend to go in goal, now you've got to score past a goalie

2 Shout where you're aiming for and go for it again

3 Use the side of your foot for accuracy, or the top for power

STAGE 4
PRO

1 Now you're ready for a penalty shoot-out

2 Ask some mates to join in and one of you has to go in goal

3 Take five penalties each and see who comes out on top!

POSITION: **Striker**
SQUAD NUMBER: 9

P

KEVIN
Phillips

Postcards from home... P

BIRMINGHAM CITY FOOTBALL CLUB - 1875 -

Sweden

NAME: Sebastian Larsson

POSITION: Midfielder

CAPITAL CITY: Stockholm.

WHERE IS IT: A Nordic country on the Scandinavian Peninsula in Northern Europe.

FAMOUS SWEDES: Inventor **Alfred Nobel**, renowned for inventing dynamite and founding the prestigious prize which bears his name - the Nobel Prize.
Björn Borg, five times Wimbledon tennis champion
Pop band **Abba**.

Serbia

NAME: Nikola Zigic

POSITION: Striker

CAPITAL CITY: Belgrade

WHERE IS IT: South Eastern Europe, surrounded by countries including Romania, Croatia, Macedonia and Hungary.

FAMOUS SERBS: Model and actress **Milla Jovovich** who has starred in films such as Zoolander and The Fifth Element. Tennis player **Novak Djokovic** and chess Grandmaster **Borislav Ivkov**.

Ireland

NAME: Keith Fahey

POSITION: Midfielder

CAPITAL CITY: Dublin

WHERE IS IT: An island across the Irish Sea from England.

FAMOUS IRISH: Rock group **U2** who've had hits such as Beautiful Day and The Sweetest Thing.
Comedian **Dara O'Briain**.
Golfer **Padraig Harrington**.

Spain

NAME: Michel

POSITION: Midfielder

CAPITAL CITY: Madrid

WHERE IS IT: Southwest Europe. Portugal is to the West, and France to the Northeast.

FAMOUS SPANIARDS:
Painters **Salvador Dalí** and **Pablo Picasso**.

Tennis Champion **Rafael Nadal**.

Pop star **Enrique Iglesias**.

Are you a brainy Blue?
Test yourself with this quick fire football quiz!

BIRMINGHAM CITY FOOTBALL CLUB - 1875 -

Q

1 Which team play their home games at the Stadium of Light?

2 How much did Real Madrid pay Manchester Utd for Ronaldo?

3 Who did the Blues play in their first home League game this season?

4 Where did Manchester City play before the City of Manchester Stadium?

5 Which Barclays Premier League boss is Frank Lampard's uncle?

6 Everton's Tim Cahill plays football for which country?

7 What is the name of the Blues training ground?

8 Which country won the 2010 World Cup?

9 How many teams are there in the Barclays Premier League?

10 Which Blues legend was the country's first £1m footballer?

_____

11 Which team did David Beckham play for before LA Galaxy?

_____

12 Who scored a hat trick for England in September's 4·0 win v Bulgaria?

_____

13 In which year did the Blues win the League Cup?

_____

14 Which team did Newcastle United hammer 6·0 in August 2010?

_____

15 Which other Premier League club has Alexander Hleb played for?

_____

16 Which football team are nicknamed the Rams?

_____

17 Steve McClaren managed which club before being England manager?

_____

18 Football team Benfica come from which country?

_____

19 Who did Inter Milan beat in the 2010 Champions League Final?

_____

20 Which team did striker Nikola Zigic join the Blues from?

_____

39

ANSWER ON PAGE 62.

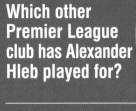

Walter Abbott

MOST GOALS IN A SEASON

42 goals · 1898-1899
34 League & 8 FA Cup

Dennis Jennings

Ian Bennett

CONSECUTIVE CLEAN SHEETS

9 · 29 October 1994
to 10 December 1994

MOST CLEAN SHEETS
IN A SEASON

27 · 1994-1995

Gil Merrick

OLDEST PLAYER

40 years 190 days
v Wolves 6 May 1950

LONGEST SERVING PLAYER

22 years · 1938–1960

MOST CLUB APPEARANCES (inc.Wartime)

713 games · 1940-1959

CONSECUTIVE APPEARANCES

145 games · 1949-1952

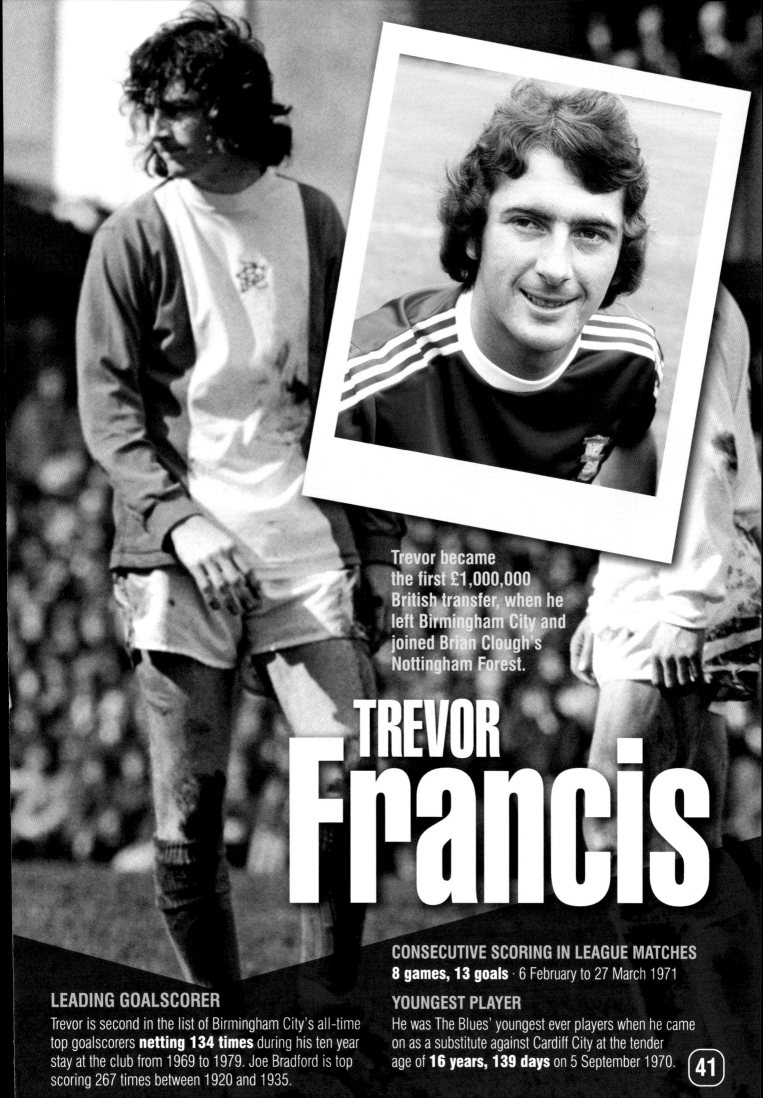

Trevor became the first £1,000,000 British transfer, when he left Birmingham City and joined Brian Clough's Nottingham Forest.

TREVOR
Francis

CONSECUTIVE SCORING IN LEAGUE MATCHES
8 games, 13 goals · 6 February to 27 March 1971

LEADING GOALSCORER
Trevor is second in the list of Birmingham City's all-time top goalscorers **netting 134 times** during his ten year stay at the club from 1969 to 1979. Joe Bradford is top scoring 267 times between 1920 and 1935.

YOUNGEST PLAYER
He was The Blues' youngest ever players when he came on as a substitute against Cardiff City at the tender age of **16 years, 139 days** on 5 September 1970.

Peter Murphy

Trevor Francis

HIGH 5

Joe Bradford holds the record having netted an incredible 267 times for the Blues in 445 games - more than one every two games!

Here are Birmingham's Top Five strikers of all time.

1	Joe Bradford	1920-1935	267 goals
2	Trevor Francis	1970-1979	134 goals
3	Peter Murphy	1952-1961	127 goals
4	Freddie Wheldon	1890-1896	118 goals
5	George Briggs	1923-1933	107 goals

Joe Bradford

George Briggs

Many prolific goalscorers have worn the blue shirt of Birmingham City FC over the years...

BIRMINGHAM CITY FOOTBALL CLUB - 1875 -

5

SPOT
the ball

The centre of the ball is in one of these squares ...but which one?

ANSWER ON PAGE 62.

GARRY O'CONNOR

KEVIN PHILLIPS

CAMERON JEROME

Being a striker has its rewards...
...but it's more about guts than glory

You have to put in the legwork to reap the benefits so here we give you some top tips for becoming a striker supreme.

1 WORK HARD!
Play your heart out right up until the final whistle, you never know when that perfect cross will come your way.

2 PASS THE BALL!
The object is for the team to score, not the individual, if someone else has a better opportunity, help them to take it.

3 DON'T SACRIFICE ACCURACY FOR POWER!
No matter how hard you kick the ball, if a shot isn't on target, it's never going in.

4 FOLLOW THROUGH!
Strike the ball with the laces of your boot and don't stop your leg motion once you've connected with the ball. If you swing your leg through it will give you more momentum.

5 KEEP SHOTS LOW & AIM FOR THE CORNERS!
These are the hardest areas for the goalie to protect.

6 PRACTISE MAKES PERFECT!
Practise shooting at a small target like a pole or tree to improve your accuracy. Gradually increase your distance from the object. Soon you'll be scoring from 25 yards!

7 ATTACK AT EVERY CHANCE YOU GET!
Make the defensive team work, the more shots you have on target, the more likely you are to score.

8 BE PATIENT!
Don't just shoot because the ball's at your feet, wait for chances, don't waste them.

9 WORK ON BOTH FEET!
Practise shooting with both your strong and weak foot, this will help make you a good all-round player, the more skilled you are, the more opportunities will present themselves.

10 HAVE CONFIDENCE IN YOURSELF!
If you get a chance, take it, if you think you can take your defender, go for it! Think fast and be decisive if you want to out-fox your opponent.

A

ETI
AIR

B

Kappa

BIRMINGHAM CITY
FOOTBALL CLUB
- 1875 -

S | You know their home colours...

C

carbrini

D

nor
re

E

F

GETTING Shirty

but do you know these Barclays Premier League teams away kits?

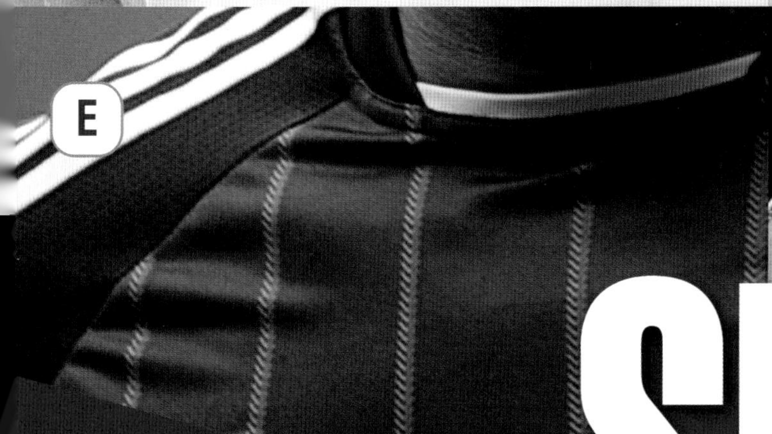

45

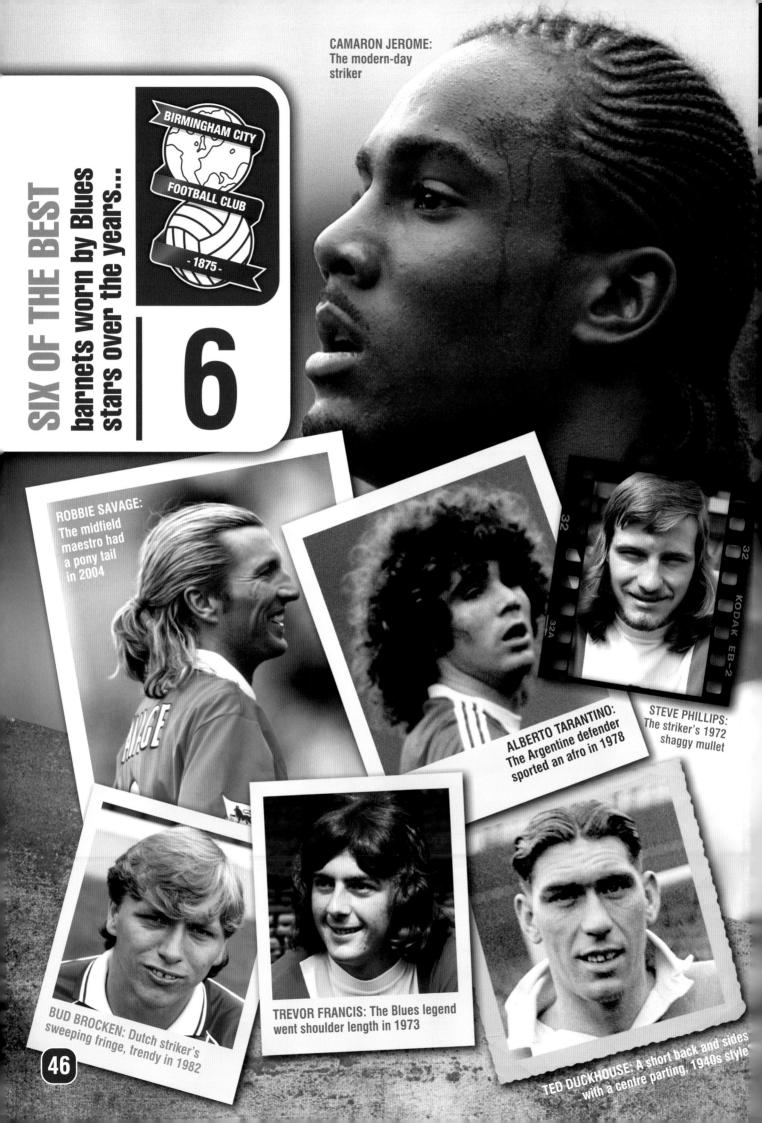

SIX OF THE BEST
barnets worn by Blues stars over the years...

6

BIRMINGHAM CITY FOOTBALL CLUB - 1875 -

CAMARON JEROME: The modern-day striker

ROBBIE SAVAGE: The midfield maestro had a pony tail in 2004

ALBERTO TARANTINO: The Argentine defender sported an afro in 1978

STEVE PHILLIPS: The striker's 1972 shaggy mullet

BUD BROCKEN: Dutch striker's sweeping fringe, trendy in 1982

TREVOR FRANCIS: The Blues legend went shoulder length in 1973

TED DUCKHOUSE: A short back and sides with a centre parting, 1940s style

46

The Northern Ireland international initially joined Blues on a season-long loan in the summer of 2003 from Fulham

POSITION: **Goalkeeper**
SQUAD NUMBER: **1**

T

Following some impressive performances, the move was made permanent in a £1.5 million deal in March 2004.

A former soldier, Taylor began his career at non-league Farnborough Town before moving into the Football League with Barnet.

After impressing in the lower divisions with the Bees, he earned a move to the Premiership with Southampton before switching to Fulham.

MAIK Taylor

CAREER:	LEAGUE	FA CUP	LEAGUE CUP
2009-10	2	-	2
2008-09	45	1	-
2007-08	34	1	-
2006-07	27	3	1
2005-06	34	6	1
2004-05	38	2	2
2003-04	34	4	1

7 STEPS...

Start by juggling the ball with your feet

Kick it a little higher than normal to give you more time to complete the move

Lift the ball with the outside of your foot, putting a slight spin on it

Continue to bring your leg round and up over the ball

AROUND THE WORLD

BIRMINGHAM CITY
FOOTBALL CLUB
- 1875 -

7

Remember...

Finally...

...and continue to juggle the ball!

...that all this should be done in one fluid motion

...bring your foot back round to your starting position

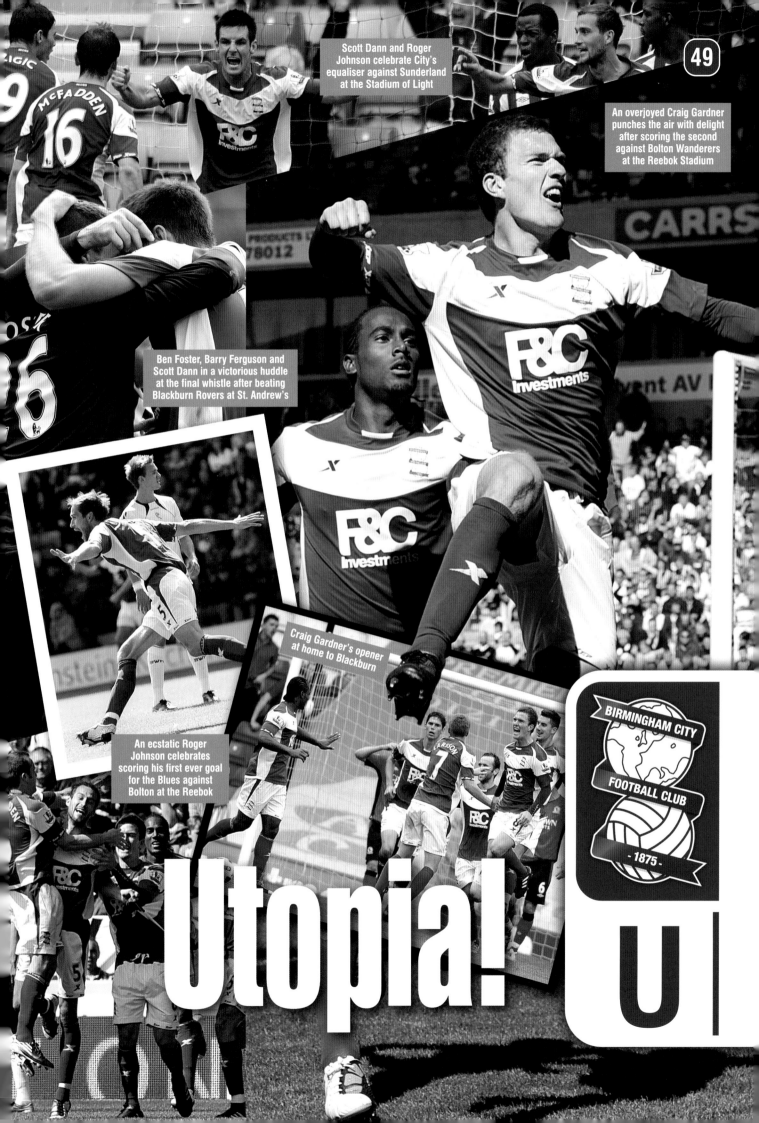

Scott Dann and Roger Johnson celebrate City's equaliser against Sunderland at the Stadium of Light

An overjoyed Craig Gardner punches the air with delight after scoring the second against Bolton Wanderers at the Reebok Stadium

Ben Foster, Barry Ferguson and Scott Dann in a victorious huddle at the final whistle after beating Blackburn Rovers at St. Andrew's

Craig Gardner's opener at home to Blackburn

An ecstatic Roger Johnson celebrates scoring his first ever goal for the Blues against Bolton at the Reebok

Utopia!

BIRMINGHAM CITY FOOTBALL CLUB - 1875 -

8

BARCLAYS PREMIER LEAGUE CHAMPIONS:

Arsenal

YOUR PREDICTION:

BARCLAYS PREMIER LEAGUE RUNNERS-UP:

Manchester United

YOUR PREDICTION:

BARCLAYS LEAGUE BOTTOM TWO:

West Ham & Newcastle Utd

YOUR PREDICTIONS: &

PREMIER LEAGUE
TOP SCORER:
Carlos Tevez

YOUR PREDICTION:

CHAMPIONS LEAGUE
WINNERS:
Chelsea

YOUR PREDICTION:

THE BLUES

CHAMPIONS LEAGUE
TOP SCORER:
Lionel Messi

YOUR PREDICTION:

FA CUP
WINNERS:
Birmingham City

YOUR PREDICTION:

4 steps...

Perfect Volley

STAGE 1
EASY PEASY

1 All you need is a football and a patch to practise in

2 Drop the ball, let it bounce, then volley it back into your hands

3 Once you start to get the hang of it, try to volley the ball without it bouncing

STAGE 2
MEDIUM

1 Ask a friend to join you and find a bit more space to play in

2 Volley the ball to your friend so they can catch it, they then volley it back to you

3 Kick it with the side or top of your foot, also try volleying without a bounce

STAGE 3
TOUGH

1 Stand a bit further apart this time and your friend starts with the ball

2 Your friend throws the ball to you and you volley it back into their hands

3 Keep practising with the top or side of your foot, swap round after five tries

STAGE 4
PRO

1 Set up a pitch with four goals, get three friends and split into teams

2 Your team mate throws you the ball and you have to score in one of the other goals

3 You win a letter every time you score a goal. First team to spell 'volley' wins!

BIRMINGHAM CITY

FOOTBALL CLUB

- 1875 -

V

...to a top class Volley!

Spot the difference

Can you spot all nine differences between these pictures?

BIRMINGHAM CITY FOOTBALL CLUB - 1875 -

9

A
- He was born in Yardley, Birmingham
- He's a lifelong Blues fan
- He signed from local rivals Aston Villa for £3m in January 2009
- He is a former England Under-21 international
- His main position is in the centre of midfield but he can also play on the right or even at right back

B
- He began his career with Walsall in 2004
- Iain Dowie signed him for Coventry in January 2008
- He joined Birmingham in June 2009
- Made his Premier League debut for the Blues in a 1-0 win at Hull
- He had a highly successful first season for the Blues alongside Roger Johnson in the centre of the Blues defence

D
- He was born 28th April 1983 in Ashford, Surrey
- He is a product of the Wycombe Wanderers youth set-up
- As well as Wycombe, he played over 100 times for Cardiff City
- He broke the Blues club transfer record paid for a defender
- As well as his defensive strength, he frequently causes opposition defences problems from set-pieces

C
- Began his football career as a schoolboy with Charlton Athletic
- He joined Leeds United in 1996 for a fee of £2.8 million
- He joined Blues on a free transfer in August 2009, after an impressive loan spell at St. Andrew's the previous season
- Whilst on loan, he scored in injury time on his debut for the Blues to secure a 1-1 draw with Cardiff City at St Andrew's
- He has played for England.

Who

W

Can you work out the identity of these Birmingham stars in as few clues as possible?

E

- He was born in Hartlepool in the North-East
- He began his career with Middlesbrough and had a loan spell at Barnsley before joining Hibernian
- He was part of the Hibernian team that won the CIS Cup 5-1 against Kilmarnock in March 2007
- He joined Blues in January 2008 for a fee of £1.5m
- He missed much of the 2009/10 season after breaking his knee cap against Watford in April 2009

are_ya

There are five clues for each player.
How many clues will you need?

ANSWERS ON PAGE 62

55

'X'word

Across

2. Johnson, Blues number 5
5. Alex's nickname, Big?
6. Number of goals in a hat-trick
7. Enric, Blues versatile spanish midfielder
8. Ben Foster plays in this position
10. The Blues 6ft 8in serbian striker
15. First name of the Blues mascot
16. Home sweet home

Down

1. City's all-time record goalscorer
2. The man supporters love to hate
3. Nathan, 16 year old young pro
4. Blues all-time record appearance maker
9. Defender signed from Coventry City in 2009
11. Keith Fahey's nationality
12. The Gaffer
13. Centre? The area of the field teams kick off
14. Birmingham City's nickname

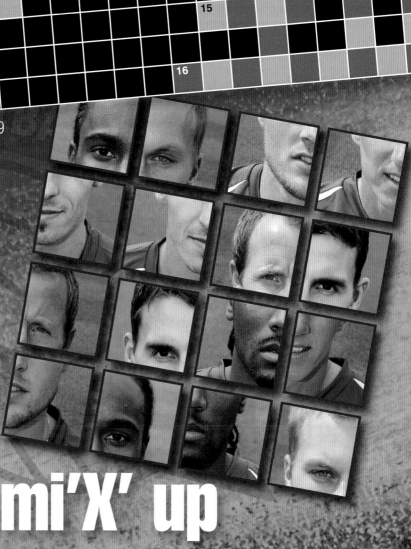

'X' FACTOR
Are you a Birmingham City 'X'pert?

BIRMINGHAM CITY FOOTBALL CLUB -1875-

X

mi'X' up

Can you identify the four Blues stars that have been mixed up in this grid?

ANSWERS ON PAGE 62

10/10

1. **Former Blues manager Steve Bruce used to play for Manchester City?**

2. **James McFadden was born in Glasgow?**

3. **Last season the Blues finished 10th in the Barclays Premier League?**

4. **Alex McLeish's nickname is Small Eck?**

5. **Blues signed England international goalkeeper Ben Foster from Manchester United in 2010?**

6. **Nikola Zigic is from Australia?**

7. **Club mascot Beau Brummie is a bulldog?**

8. **Scott Dann joined the Blues from Aston Villa?**

9. **Blues 1st game of the 2010-11 season was a 2-2 draw against Sunderland at The Stadium of Light?**

10. **James Phelps, Harry Potter's Fred Weasley, is a Birmingham City fan?**

ANSWERS ON PAGE 62

BIRMINGHAM CITY FOOTBALL CLUB - 1875 -

10

Can you work out the answers to these true or false questions? WRITE A 'T' OR 'F' IN THE BOXES!

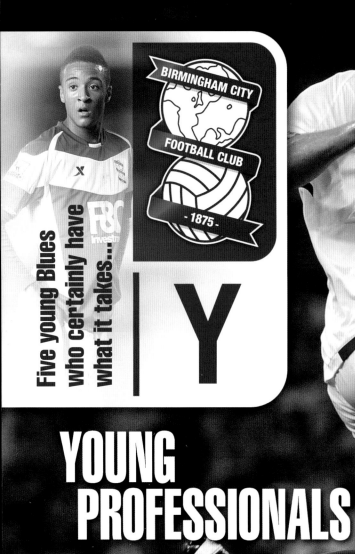

Five young Blues who certainly have what it takes...

Y

YOUNG PROFESSIONALS

Jordon Mutch

Highly rated 18-year-old midfielder Jordon Mutch spent much of the 2009-10 campaign out on loan gaining valuable first team experience with Hereford United and Doncaster Rovers.

He went out on loan again at the start of the 2010-11 season, when he joined Championship side Watford.

Nathan Redmond

A tricky, pacey winger, 16-year-old Nathan's qualities were recognised by Alex McLeish when he was given his first team debut v Rochdale in Carling Cup Round 2, at just 16 years and 173 days, making him the second youngest debutant behind Blues legend Trevor Francis.

He is an England U17 international

Fraser Kerr

Scottish defender Kerr signed from Motherwell in the summer of 2009 as a first year scholar.

The 17-year-old centre back has represented his country right up to U19 level.

He was included in the first team squad for the club's Far East in the summer of 2010.

Jack Butland

One of the best young goalkeepers in the country, Bristol-born Butland tasted international success in the summer of 2010 when he helped England U17s to European glory.

His fine performances for the Three Lions saw him rewarded with his U19s debut in September.

Jake Jervis

Signed form Shrewsbury Town at the age of 15, the striker was top scorer for both the Academy and Reserve sides in the 2009-10 season. During that season he was made his first team debut as a late sub in an FA Cup tie at Everton.

He joined Notts County on loan at the start of the 2010-11 season.

BIRMINGHAM CITY FOOTBALL CLUB
- 1875 -

Z

POSITION: Striker
SQUAD NUMBER: 19

F&C Investments

NIKOLA ZIGIC

St.Andrew's has seen a legion of talent in its time. Here is our dream team... see if you agree!

11

NAME:
Roger Johnson

PLAYED FOR BLUES:
2009-date

POSITION:
Defender

FACT:
Causes problems with his aerial ability from set prices

MY CHOICE:

NAME:
Jeff Hall

PLAYED FOR BLUES:
1950-1959

POSITION:
Defender

FACT:
Classy and consistent right back

MY CHOICE:

NAME:
Howard Kendall

PLAYED FOR BLUES:
1974-1977

POSITION:
Midfielder

FACT:
Simply one of the best midfield players of his generation

MY CHOICE:

NAME:
Trevor Francis

PLAYED FOR BLUES:
1970-1979

POSITION:
Striker

FACT:
Arguably Blues best ever player - fast, skillful and lethal

MY CHOICE:

BLUES firsteleven

NAME:
Gil Merrick

PLAYED FOR BLUES:
1938-1960

POSITION:
Goalkeeper

FACT:
Blues longest serving player and record appearance maker

MY CHOICE:

NAME:
Steve Bruce

PLAYED FOR BLUES:
1996-1998

POSITION:
Defender

FACT:
Tough tackling defender and superb in the air

MY CHOICE:

NAME:
Martin Grainger

PLAYED FOR BLUES:
1996-2005

POSITION:
Defender

FACT:
Tough,passionate and also had a magic left foot

MY CHOICE:

NAME:
Christophe Dugarry

PLAYED FOR BLUES:
2003-2004

POSITION:
Striker

FACT:
Sublime touch and vision.Gained iconic status at St.Andrew's

MY CHOICE:

NAME:
Craig Gardner

PLAYED FOR BLUES:
2009-date

POSITION:
Midfielder

FACT:
Versatile midfielder who can also play as a right winger

MY CHOICE:

NAME:
Geoff Horsfield

PLAYED FOR BLUES:
2000-2003

POSITION:
Striker

FACT:
Strong and forceful player

MY CHOICE:

NAME:
Alex Govan

PLAYED FOR BLUES:
1953-1958

POSITION:
Left Winger

FACT:
Scored five hat-tricks for Blues in the 1956-57 season

MY CHOICE:

Answers

Page 9: Club Crest Test
A. Wolves. B. Manchester Utd. C. Bolton.
D. Arsenal. E. Sunderland. F. Spurs

Page 14: Stars in their Eyes
A. Scott Dann. B. Matt Derbyshire.
C. Nikola Zigic. D. Roger Johnson.
E. Sebastian Larsson. F. Lee Bowyer.
G. Kevin Phillips. H. Barry Ferguson.

Page 16: Fan'tastic
Ronaldinho, David Beckham, Andy Murray,
Shaun White and Steve Davis.

Page 21: Take 2
Kevin Phillips and Roger Johnson. James McFadden and Barry Ferguson.

Page 22: Internationals
Belarus: Alexander Hleb. Chile: Jean Beausejour. Czech Republic: Martin Jiranek.
England: Ben Foster, Kevin Phillips and Lee Bowyer. Northern Ireland: Maik Taylor
and Colin Doyle. Republic of Ireland: Stephen Carr and Keith Fahey.
Scotland: James McFadden, Barry Ferguson and Garry O'Connor. Serbia: Nikola Zigic.
Sweden: Sebastian Larsson.

Page 28: Mega Pixels
A. Sebastian Larsson. B. Barry Ferguson. C. Roger Johnson. D. Cameron Jerome.
E. Liam Ridgewell.

Page 38: Quick Fire
1. Sunderland. 2. £80million. 3. Blackburn Rovers. 4. Maine Road. 5. Harry Redknapp.
6. Australia. 7. Wast Hills. 8. Spain. 9. 20. 10. Trevor Francis. 11. Real Madrid.
12. Jermain Defoe. 13. 1963. 14. Aston Villa. 15. Arsenal. 16. Derby County.
17. Middlesbrough. 18. Portugal. 19, Bayern Munich. 20. Valencia.

Page 43: Spot the Ball - See below

Page 43: Spot the Difference - See below

Page 56: 'X'word - See below

Page 56: Mi'X' up
Sebastian Larsson, Matt Derbyshire, Lee Bowyer
and Cameron Jerome

Page 57: 10/10 True or False
1. False - Manchester Utd. 2. True. 3. False - 9th.
4. False - Big Eck. 5.True. 6. False - Serbia. 7. True.
8. False - Coventry City. 9. True. 10. True.